EYE-LOOK
Picture Games

Look and Compare

A Photo Analogy Game

by Kristen McCurry

CAPSTONE PRESS
a capstone imprint

A+ books are published by Capstone Press,
1710 Roe Crest Drive, North Mankato, Minnesota 56003.
www.capstonepub.com

Books published by Capstone Press are manufactured with paper containing at least 10 percent post-consumer waste.

Library of Congress Cataloging-in-Publication Data
McCurry, Kristen.
  Look and compare : a photo analogy game / by Kristen McCurry.
     p. cm.—(A+ books. Eye-look picture games)
  Includes bibliographical references.
  Summary: "Simple text invites readers to sort groups of objects in full-color photos"—Provided by publisher.
  ISBN 978-1-4296-7551-2 (library binding)
  1. Picture puzzles—Juvenile literature. I. Title. II. Series.
  GV1507.P47M375 2012
  793.73—dc23   2011043259

Credits

Jeni Wittrock, editor; Tracy Davies McCabe, designer; Marcie Spence, media researcher; Laura Manthe, production specialist; Sarah Schuette, photo stylist; Marcy Morin, studio scheduler

Photo Credits

Capstone Studio: Karon Dubke, 10 (bottom), 11 (bottom), 24, (bottom), 27 (top); iStockphoto: DonNichols, 17 (top), roseburn, 29 (bottom); Shutterstock: Adisa, cover (top left), 22 (bottom), Africa Studio, 14 (bottom), 25 (bottom), Alex Staroseltsev, 30 (middle), Anatoliy Samara, 5 (bottom), Andreas Gradin, 21 (top), Andrey.Tiyk, 7, Arkady, 20 (top left), AVAVA, 24 (top left), c., 29 (top), Chesapeake Images, 23 (bottom), cynoclub, cover (bottom right), Eric Isselee, 30 (bottom left), Darrin henry, 24 (top right), David Lee, 8 (top right), DenisNata, 4 (bottom), deva, 5 (middle), Dudarev Mikhail, 6 (bottom), Eduardo Rivero, cover (bottom left), gameanna, 6 (top right), 23 (top), George Dolgikh, 13 (bottom), George Toubalis, cover (top right), 22 (top right), gosphotodesign, 27 (middle), Gucio_55, 21 (middle), hkann, 30 (bottom right), inxti, 26 (top right), Joel Blit, 25 (middle), Joshua Haviv, 28 (bottom), Kitch Bain, 13 (top and middle), Lindsay McWilliams, 4 (top left), Lorraine Swanson, 9 (middle), Magone, 17 (middle), Maksim Toome, 12 (bottom), martin, 16 (bottom), Matej Ziak, 20 (bottom), matka_Wariatka, 16 (top right), Michael Pettigrew, 9 (bottom), Mike Flippo, 15 (top), Nadezda, 10 (top right), newphotoservice, 25 (top), Nikolai Pozdeev, 4 (top right), oriontrail, 28 (top left), Panom, 29 (middle), PedroClipArt, 26 (bottom), Philip Lange, 11 (middle), Poulsons Photography, 5 (top), RCPPhoto, 8 (top left), Robyn Mackenzie, 14 (top right), 15 (bottom), S. Matveev, 14 (top left), Sarah Holmlund, 22 (top left), Scorpp, 23 (middle), Serg64, 6 (top left), Shawn Hempel, 21 (bottom), shutswis, 8 (bottom), Songquan Deng, 28 (top right), steamroller_blues, 12 (top left), Steven Frame, 11 (top), stocksnapp, 26 (top left), sunsetman, 10 (top left), tarasov, 20 (top right), Tihis, 12 (top right), Vaclav Volrab, 9 (top), VIPDesignUSA, 17 (bottom), Workmans Photos, 27 (bottom), yeo2205, 16 (top left), ZouZou, 30 (top)

Note to Parents, Teachers, and Librarians

The Eye-Look Picture Games series supports national math standards related to grouping and sorting and national language arts standards related to the use of comparisons and analogies. The images support early readers in understanding the text. The repetition of words and phrases helps early readers learn new words. Early readers may need assistance to read some words and to use the Read More and Internet Sites sections of the book.

Printed in the United States of America in North Mankato, Minnesota.
102011   006405CGS12

Analogies!

The puzzles in this book are analogies.
A-nala-what? Ah-nal-uh-jeez! In an analogy,
you compare things.

How does it work?

First, look carefully at two pictures. Ask yourself:
how are these pictures related? What's their
connection? Then try to find the same kind of
connection between a second set of pictures.

Sometimes the answers seem easy. You figure them
out in a flash. But sometimes you have to flip your
brain inside out! Turn the page and give it a try.

Answer key on page 31

Tail is to wag

as

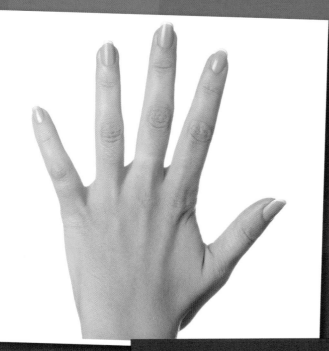

?

hand is to _____.

4

Tail and wag. How are those words connected? A dog would use a tail to wag, right?

OK, look at the next line. Hand. Which of the pictures is related to hand the way that tail is related to wag?

ring

finger

wave

Not *ring*. That's something you wear. Not *finger*. That's part of your hand.

Wave. There you go! That's something you do with your hand. Just like wagging is something a dog does with its tail. That's your analogy!

Sky is to blue

as

grass is to _____.

red

lawnmower

green

Bat is to ball

as

?

hockey stick is to _____.

8

puck

face mask

goalie net

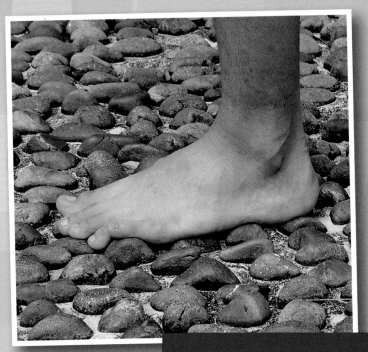

Foot is to shoe

as

_____ is to helmet.

elbow

hand

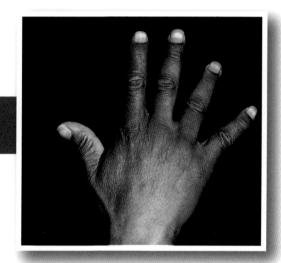

head

Bike is to two wheels

as

?

car is to _____.

four wheels

three wheels

steering wheel

Pizza is to circle

as

sandwich is to _____.

lunch

square

triangle

Strawberries are to jam as

peanuts are to _____.

16

peanut butter

bread

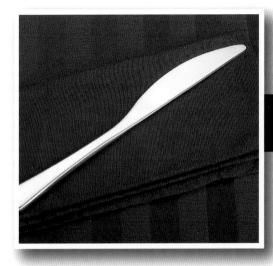

knife

Square is to four

as

triangle is to _____.

18

2 two

circle

3 three

Seedling is to tree

as

?

tadpole is to _____.

fish

frog

pond

Fish is to water

as

_____ is to sky.

blue

dog

bird

Teacher is to school

as

doctor is to _____.

library

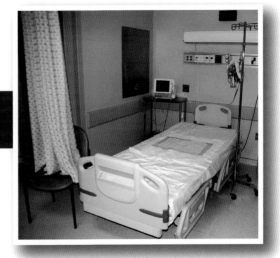

hospital

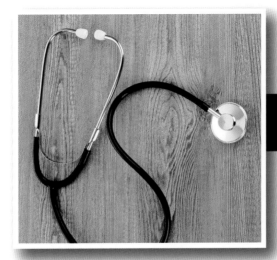

stethoscope

Shovel is to dirt

as

_____ is to food.

hammer

spoon

banana

Sun is to day

as

? _____ is to night.

moon

cloud

bed

How did you do on these analogies? Did you find the connections between the pictures?

Analogies make you think in different ways. Look at the answer key on the next page to check your work. But first, here's one final analogy for you to solve:

Exercise is to your body

as

analogies are to your _____!

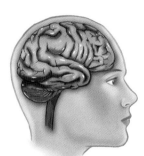

Answer Key

Pages 6-7 green

Pages 8-9 puck

Pages 10-11 head

Pages 12-13 four wheels

Pages 14-15 square

Pages 16-17 peanut butter

Pages 18-19 three

Pages 20-21 frog

Pages 22-23 bird

Pages 24-25 hospital

Pages 26-27 spoon

Pages 28-29 moon

Page 30 brain

Read More

Barnhill, Kelly Regan. *Guess What's Growing: A Photo Riddle Book.* Nature Riddles. Mankato, Minn.: Capstone Press, 2010.

Kalz, Jill. *An A-maze-ing Amusement Park Adventure.* A-maze-ing Adventures. Mankato, Minn.: Picture Window Books, 2011.

Staake, Bob. *Look! A Book!* New York: Little, Brown, 2011.

Internet Sites

FactHound offers a safe, fun way to find Internet sites related to this book. All of the sites on FactHound have been researched by our staff.

Here's all you do:

Visit www.facthound.com

Type in this code: 9781429675512

Check out projects, games and lots more at
www.capstonekids.com